ANCIENT EGYPTIAN
WONDERS

Life Along the Ancient Nile

Jim Whiting

ReferencePoint Press®

San Diego, CA

LIBRARY OF CONGRESS CATALOGING-IN-PUBLICATION DATA

Whiting, Jim, 1951-
 Life along the ancient Nile / by Jim Whiting.
   p. cm. -- (Ancient Egyptian wonders series)
 Includes bibliographical references and index.
 ISBN 978-1-60152-252-8 (hardback : alk. paper) -- ISBN 1-60152-252-5 (hardback : alk. paper)
 1. Egypt--Civilization--To 332 B.C. 2. Nile River Valley--Civilization. I. Title. II. Series: Ancient Egyptian wonders series.
 DT61.W483 2013
 932.01--dc23
                                                              2012000358

CONTENTS

A TIMELINE OF ANCIENT EGYPT

Editor's note: Dates for major events and periods in ancient Egyptian history vary widely. Dates used here coincide with a timeline compiled by John Baines, professor of Egyptology at University of Oxford in England.

Great Pyramids of Giza are built by Khufu, Khafre, and Menkaure.

First pyramid, the Step Pyramid at Saqqara, is built by Djoser.

Capital city of Memphis is founded.

Upper and Lower Egypt unify as one kingdom.

Late Predynastic Period (ca. 3100–2950 BC)

Early Dynastic Period (ca. 2950–2575 BC)

Old Kingdom (ca. 2575–2150 BC)

First Intermediate Period (ca. 2125–1975 BC)

Middle Kingdom (ca. 1975–1640 BC)

Hieroglyphic script is developed.

Old Kingdom collapses, resulting in a period of social upheaval and political chaos.

Egypt prospers during its classical period of art and literature.

Mentuhotep reunites Egypt.

Egypt enjoys peace for more than 50 years under Ramesses II, a noted warrior and prolific builder.

Ptolemy becomes king after Alexander's death in 323 BC; he founds a dynasty that rules Egypt for nearly three centuries.

The Rosetta stone, which later provides the key to deciphering Egyptian hieroglyphs, is carved.

Tutankhamun (King Tut) dies at a young age after a short reign; his undisturbed tomb is discovered in the Valley of the Kings in AD 1922.

Egypt regains its independence.

Hyksos rulers are driven from Egypt.

Persians conquer Egypt.

Hyksos kings invade and seize power in Egypt.

Nubians conquer Egypt.

Second Intermediate Period (ca. 1630–1520 BC)

New Kingdom (ca. 1539–1075 BC)

Third Intermediate Period (ca. 1075–715 BC)

Late Period (715–332 BC)

Greco-Roman Period (332 BC– AD 395)

Akhenaten introduces an unpopular monotheistic religion.

Alexander the Great conquers Egypt and makes it part of his vast empire.

Egypt is ruled by Hatshepsut, a woman pharaoh.

Cleopatra VII (better known as Cleopatra) serves as Egypt's last independent ruler.

Egypt becomes a province of the Roman Empire in 30 BC.

INTRODUCTION

The Gift of
the Nile

Every year, in mid- to late July, the people of ancient Egypt began scanning the skies for the reappearance of Sothis, the star we know today as Sirius, the Dog Star. No one could miss it. It was—and is—the brightest star in the sky.

Within a few days after its return, the Egyptians knew that one of the most predictable—and vital—events affecting their lives and well-being would occur. The Nile River—alongside which nearly everyone lived—would begin rising. Soon it would overflow its banks, burying both sides of the river beneath a sheet of several feet of water that extended inland for several miles. An ancient Greek named Herodotus, who is often called the "father of history," had traveled to Egypt sometime between 460 and 450 BC and had observed this flooding. While historians question some of his accounts of life in the ancient world, they generally regard his observations of Egyptian life as accurate. At the peak of the river's flooding, he noted, "all of Egypt becomes like a sea, except for the cities which alone project above water, quite like the islands in the Aegean Sea."[1]

> **DID YOU KNOW?**
> Originally, the Egyptians simply referred to the Nile as *iteru*, or "the great river." Nile comes from the Greek word *neilo*, or "water."

Unlike the Aegean Islands, however, this condition was temporary. Within two months the waters would recede, and eventually the Nile would return to its former level. The flood left behind something priceless: dark, nutrient-rich silt the floodwaters had carried with them. This silt provided natural fertilizer that—in conjunction with virtually year-round sunshine—allowed Egyptian farmers to grow bountiful crops in an otherwise barren desert. These crops were the basis for the development of a thriving, prosperous civilization, which provided one of the ancient world's highest standards of living and influenced virtually every aspect of daily life. No wonder, then, that to Herodotus, this "land that was deposited by the river—it is the gift of the river to the Egyptians."[2]

The ebb and flow of daily life in ancient Egypt revolved around the annual flooding of the Nile River (pictured). Bathed by the desert sun, the nutrient-rich silt deposited along the riverbanks produced bountiful harvests and provided the basis for a thriving civilization.

THE NILE'S OTHER GIFTS

The Nile offered other gifts as well: fresh water for bathing, an easy and reliable method for transportation and trade, mud to construct houses and public buildings, clay for ceramics, the reeds and leaves of riverside date palms for baskets, papyrus plants for making boats and a form of paper, abundant fish and waterfowl for the dinner table, and more.

As a result, ancient Egypt was divided into *kemet*, or Black Land (the narrow fertile strip along the Nile, so called because of the dark color of the sediment that blanketed the land as the river receded), and *deret*, or Red Land (apart from a few oases, the surrounding desert). As historian Jason Thompson notes, "A view of the Nile Valley from the air is unforgettable: a band of intense green running through a desolate desert. The contrast can also be striking on the ground, where one can literally stand with one foot in fertile fields and the other on barren sand."[3]

> **DID YOU KNOW?**
> The Egyptians developed an early calendar based on the Nile. The year was divided into three equal parts: *akhet* (inundation), *peret* (growing), and *shemu* (harvesting).

Despite its obvious value to them, the Egyptians had no idea what produced this annual bounty. Roman leader Julius Caesar, who spent several years in Egypt, was similarly perplexed. "Nothing would satisfy my intellectual curiosity more fully than to be told what makes the Nile rise,"[4] he said.

ONE RIVER, TWO BRANCHES

The natural forces that brought this annual gift to Egypt are well understood today. The Nile actually has two branches: the White Nile and the Blue Nile, which meet near Khartoum in modern-day Sudan. The White Nile rises near Lake Victoria in central Africa and has a very consistent annual flow, which stays well within its banks. The situation is very different with the Blue Nile. For much of the year, it is little more than a trickle. Things change dramatically in June, when heavy monsoon rains from the Indian Ocean sweep into the Ethiopi-

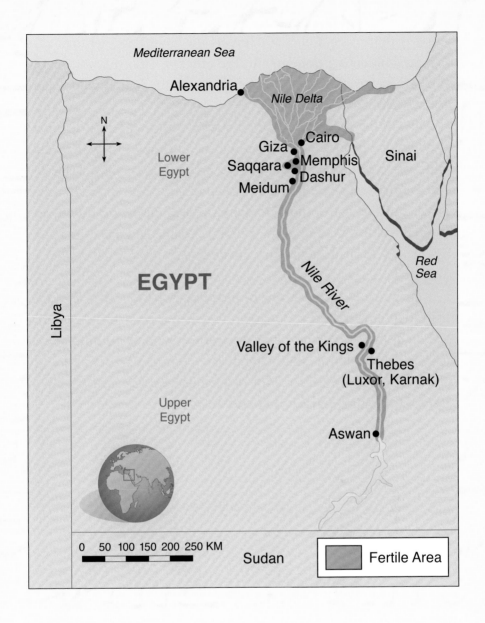

an highlands, southeast of Egypt. These rains pour into the Blue Nile, accounting for most of the water that heads downstream and reaches Egypt in early August. The floodwaters peak in September, with as much as five or six times the river's flow in June. The flow drops off sharply after that, returning to normal levels by December.

The Nile flooded every year, and sometimes it could flood too much. If that happened, the walls surrounding many towns could be breached, destroying homes and leaving the ground soggier than usual, thereby hindering crop growth. The situation was even worse if the flood was low. Few crops could be grown in the barren sand. Many people could starve.

Most of the time, though, the flooding was predictable. This predictability led to a strong belief in routine in people's daily lives. This belief was called *maat*. According to archaeologist Joyce Tyldesley, maat is "a concept of 'rightness' that embraced ideas of truth, order, justice, and the status quo."[5] Its opposite was chaos, confusion, and disorder, and it was so important that it became embodied in a goddess named Maat. Her primary attribute was the ostrich feather of truth on her head.

Adherence to maat was one of the primary reasons that Egyptian civilization endured for so long and why it was so stable. According to Thompson, "[Egyptians'] lives were often harsh, sometimes not far above bare subsistence even in good times, but they lived in a society suffused by maat, in which all of its members experienced a sense of place, of belonging, and felt they had some stake, however small."[6]

CHAPTER 1

Home and Family Life

The history of ancient Egyptian civilization focuses on *kemet*, the Black Land, which was the inhabited portion. *Deret*, or the Red Land—the surrounding desert—also played a key role in Egypt's growth and development. It was the source of minerals used to make tools that many craftspeople used on a daily basis and provided building materials for public projects such as pyramids and temples. The desert's extreme dryness preserved monuments and mummies, thereby providing historians with a great amount of information they would not otherwise have had. In addition, the miles of shifting sands provided a buffer against invasion and interference from other countries.

Shut away from the outside world, Egypt worked out its own way of life. Today many people find that way of life one of the most fascinating of all ancient cultures. While mummies and pyramids are the most obvious sources of interest, daily life in ancient Egypt also fascinates many—as it has for many centuries.

Writing nearly two and a half millennia ago, Herodotus was as far removed from the dim past of Egypt as we are from his own times. Yet he had the same fascination as we have today. "I am going to extend my account of Egypt at some length here and give additional details about it, because this country has more marvels and monuments that defy description than any other,"[7] he wrote.

Egyptians themselves were enamored of their own past. Khaemwise, son of the great king Ramesses II, traveled to the pyramids at Giza, built more than 1,000 years before his own time. Writing in the third person, he noted that "it was the High Priest and Prince Khaemwise who delighted in this statue of the king's son Kawab, which he discovered. . . . He loved the noble ones who dwelt in antiquity before him, and the excellence of everything they made."[8]

This excellence endured despite major upheavals such as the First and Second Intermediate Periods, when political order disintegrated and introduced periods of civil war. Yet these outbreaks did not really influence underlying patterns of daily life, which remained almost unchanged for more than 3,000 years.

Over thousands of years the dry desert air helped to preserve ancient Egypt's grand structures and the mummified remains of rulers such as Ramesses the Great (displayed at Cairo's Egyptian Museum). Experts have been able to learn much about ancient Egyptian civilization from these and other artifacts.

FAMILY STRUCTURE

The basic unit of Egyptian daily life was the family, based on the union of a husband and a wife. Usually, both partners came from the same social level. Typically, the husband worked outside the home, and the wife managed the household. In farming families, for example, the husband worked in the fields, and his children often helped out as well. His wife cooked meals, kept the house clean, made and mended clothing, did laundry, and so on.

Typically, Egyptians married at a much younger age than most people today. Girls might become wives as early as age 10, though waiting until they reached sexual maturity—usually 12 or 13—was far more common. Boys usually waited a few years longer, primarily so they would be able to afford the expenses connected with marriage: a house, its furnishings, and a reasonable expectation of caring for family members. About 2400 BC, an important official named Ptahhotep wrote, "If you have already made yourself a name, then start a family."[9] With an average life expectancy of less than 40 years, there was little or no point in delaying.

LOVE OF CHILDREN

Unlike contemporary society, deciding not to have children was not really an option. Egyptians seem to have genuinely cared for their offspring. Some other ancient cultures practiced exposure, in which unwanted babies—usually girls—were taken out at night and left to die, either from freezing to death or being devoured by marauding animals. The Egyptians would have considered this the height of barbarism. They lost enough children through disease.

It seems clear that there was a preference for having boys, or at least one to carry on the family name and business. According to the *Instruction of Hardjedef*, an early guide for proper behavior:

When you prosper, found your household,
Take a hearty wife, a son will be born you.
It is for the son you build a house.[10]

Another behavior guide, the *Instruction of Ankhshosheng*, makes the same point and even provides an exact age for marriage: "Marry at 20, so that you can have a son while you are still young."[11]

In most cases Egyptians chose their own spouses. Normally the consent of the bride's father was essential. If he was dead or otherwise absent, an uncle would usually step in. In some cases, most often involving the nobility and the desire to connect important families, marriages might be arranged.

MARRIAGE AND FAMILY

Because of this freedom of choice, most marriages seem to have involved couples who genuinely loved each other. As longtime archaeology writer Ilene Springer notes, "Museums are filled with statues and paintings showing husbands and wives with their arms around each other's waists, holding hands or offering each other flowers or food. Love and affection was indeed a part of the Egyptian marriage, and our Egyptian bride could expect to be loved and respected by her husband."[12] Numerous tombstones showing husbands and wives smiling and holding each other demonstrate that couples did not believe that their love would end with death.

> **DID YOU KNOW?**
> Herodotus said that Egyptians purged themselves every month by vomiting and using enemas as a way of cleansing their systems.

Ptahhotep provides more evidence for this belief:

When you prosper and found your house,
And love your wife with ardor,
Fill her belly, clothe her back,
Gladden her heart as long as you live.[13]

There was no formal marriage ceremony, and marriage itself had no religious significance. The bride simply moved to her new husband's home. The Egyptians did, however, enjoy having a good time. Most marriages involved a substantial feast. Music, dancing, and other forms of merrymaking continued well into the night.

Often a scribe—an educated official who knew how to write—drew up a contract between the husband and wife. Poorer couples did not have contracts since the expense of hiring a scribe was too great.

Dating from the fourth century BC, a marriage contract between two young people named Herakleides and Demetria is similar to countless other documents. Though their heritage was Greek, the young couple and their families had settled in the Egyptian town of Elephantine, far up the Nile River. The contract states:

> Herakleides, a free man, takes Demetria, a free woman of Cos, as his legitimate wife from her father Leptines of Cos and from her mother Philotis, bringing clothing and jewelry (worth) 1000 drachmas. Let Herakleides provide to Demetria everything pertaining to a free wife. . . .
>
> If Demetria is discovered doing any evil to the shame of her husband Herakleides, let her be deprived of everything she brought (to the marriage); but let Herakleides prove whatever he sues Demetria about before three men on whom they both agree.
>
> Herakleides shall not be permitted to bring in another woman as an outrage to Demetria, nor have children by another woman, nor deal deceitfully in any way on any pretense, Herakleides against Demetria. If Herakleides is discovered doing any of these things and Demetria proves it before three men whom they both designate, Herakleides shall return the dowry of 1000 drachmas to Demetria which she brought and let him indemnify her in addition with 1000 drachmas of the silver (coinage) of Alexander.[14]

Because of their desire to have children, Egyptians welcomed pregnancy but recognized that it was fraught with dangers. Infant mortality was high, and the first year or two of a newborn's life were quite perilous. A graveside inscription indicated the sad fate of a young woman named Herois:

> Heavy wombed
> In pained labor she set down her burden,
> Mother was she for a moment, the child perished also.
> What was the luckless one's age?—Two times nine
> Years of flowering youth had Herois.[15]

Accordingly, many religious rites were connected with the effort to ensure a safe pregnancy and successful birth. Most women took care of their own children after birth, carrying them around and breast-feeding them. Wealthy Egyptians often hired servants to perform those tasks.

MUD-BRICK HOMES

Egyptian family life centered around their homes. The size of the dwellings varied with socioeconomic status, though nearly all were made of mud bricks because of the proximity to the Nile River.

To construct a home, builders hauled copious quantities of river mud to the site, then combined it with small amounts of straw and poured the mixture into wooden molds. The molds were placed in direct sunlight, where the mixture dried to the consistency of clay. Then the bricks were removed from the molds and used to construct walls. The roof consisted of rushes covered with plaster.

When the job was completed, the exterior was whitewashed to reflect the fierce sun. The interior walls might also be painted, and if the family could afford it, they could have decorative murals. A few small, grated openings were placed high up the walls for privacy and to prevent dust and the ever-present sand from seeping inside. Several vents on the roof were angled to catch the wind and provide circulation of air within the house.

TOILETS AND SANITATION

A few wealthy homes may have had some type of primitive toilets, as archaeological evidence shows an early version of sit-down toilets dating back more than 4,000 years. The people who lived in these homes would relieve themselves in small toilet rooms, and the waste would be carried away either by dumping buckets of water on it or by running water from nearby canals. It could also drain directly into a sand-filled container, which a servant would empty from time to time.

A more typical household would have an open pit or some kind of container. When the receptacle became full, the waste matter would be emptied into the river or open trenches in the streets.

The Egyptians liked to keep clean. Homes might contain bathrooms, which had a square piece of limestone in the corner with short walls on two or more sides. The master of the house or his wife would stand in the center while servants poured water over them. The water would drain through a trough in the limestone into earthenware bowls, which would be emptied outside the house.

While wealthy people had large homes with many rooms, a typical home for most people was relatively small and consisted of just 3 to 4 rooms. There was a small entry room and a much larger main room, where the roof was raised to admit more light. This room was the primary living space, where the family spent the majority of its time and probably ate its meals. It often had a niche where small statues of household gods would be kept. Behind the main room was a smaller room that could serve as a bedroom, though families often slept in the main room as well. Typically, the kitchen was an adjacent enclosed area with the roof left open to allow the heat and cooking odors to escape. In a climate in which daytime temperatures could rise above 100°F (38°C) in the summer and 65°F (18°C) during winter, there was no need for the extra heat of a cooking fire or hot coals.

Most homes also had a basement, which typically consisted of one or two small rooms. This not only conserved living space but also provided a slightly cooler area for storage. There were stairs or ramps to the roof for additional living and sleeping space. Townhouses for craftsmen might have two stories. The craftsman conducted his business on the ground floor, with the second floor serving as living quarters.

FURNISHINGS

Most houses had little furniture, and those items were relatively small. Even the dining area contained several smaller tables, so people could eat singly or in pairs. A few small stools were probably scattered around the rooms. Since most people had few possessions, a chest or two and some baskets for storage held everything they did not need right away. Homes might also have oil lamps, though oil was expensive and most people went to bed at sunset and were up by sunrise.

Wealthier Egyptians had beds that consisted of wooden frames with woven cords or leather strips to support the sleepers and were covered with linen sheets. Beds sloped gently downward, so a footboard prevented anyone from sliding off. They used headrests, which most commonly were made of wood, stone, pottery, or similar materials and appear to have been very uncomfortable. Nearly everyone else slept on the floor on thin mattresses, which were rolled up in the morning.

There was hardly anything else in the bedroom. A few boxes and chests would hold extra clothing, and a low table could be used for toilet articles.

DIET AND COOKING

In ancient Egypt, bread was essential to life. Each morning, women ground emmer wheat or barley on a flat stone using rollers. When the flour was fine enough, they would mix it with yeast and water. Frequently, flavors such as honey or spices were added to the mixture, which was then left to rise. When it was ready, the dough was put into two-piece clay pots and placed on a bed of glowing coals. It was taken from the coals at the right time and served fresh and piping hot.

The daily bread-baking ritual began each morning with the grinding of wheat or barley. The finely ground flour would then be mixed with water and yeast. Wooden figurines from a Middle Kingdom–era tomb depict bread bakers at work.

DEIR EL-MEDINA

Unlike the stone pyramids and temples, few traces remain of houses and other structures built of mud bricks. A notable exception is Deir el-Medina, a village housing craftspeople who worked on the tombs of Egyptian kings between about 1500 and 1000 BC. A wall encircled the town, with a single gate opening onto the main street, which was about 5 feet (1.5m) wide. Originally, the village contained about 70 houses, with another 40 added later. So that the artisans could focus their energy on their jobs, servants and slaves living outside the wall provided them with the necessities of life. In addition, the workers received regular rations of wheat, barley, and beer.

Besides the ruins, archaeologists have uncovered a great deal of written material that provides information about the daily lives of the inhabitants. For example, one man missed work one day because he had a fight with his wife. Another man stayed out late drinking with a friend and was too hungover to report to his job the next day. And one night a worker chased his stepfather through the streets, screaming that he wanted to kill the man. He did not.

Because fresh water was almost always riddled with bacteria and nasty parasites, virtually everyone—regardless of age—drank beer. It became the other basic staple of the Egyptian diet. In fact, the Egyptian symbol for *meal* is a combination of the signs of bread and beer. Horst Dornbusch of *BeerAdvocate* magazine notes that while beer was actually invented in ancient Sumer about 1,000 years before the Egyptians, "the Egyptians left us with the best documentation of ancient brewing practices. Most of the many depictions of Egyptian brewing that have come down to us are murals in vaults, pyramids, and sacrificial chambers. These attest to the importance and high esteem in which the art of beer-making was held in Egyptian society."[16]

To produce beer, chunks of barley bread were crumbled into a large vat of water, then sweetened with honey or sweet fruits such as dates to form a mash, which was poured into large crocks. After fermenting, the mixture was strained into jars, sealed, and stored. Unlike our era, beer was usually served warm. What little wine was produced was largely for the wealthy.

Egyptians ate a variety of vegetables, such as beans, lentils, and onions. There was also milk and cheese. While meat came from a variety of sources—such as cattle, sheep, goats, pigs, chickens, ducks, and even hyenas and other wild animals—it was usually reserved for the well-to-do. They normally regarded fish from the Nile as unclean, though it provided valuable protein for farmers. And as Herodotus observed, "There are other people in the marshes who live only on the fish that they catch; they remove the guts, dry the fish in the sun, and eat them."[17]

> **DID YOU KNOW?**
> Faced with the possibility of baldness, some men tried to restore hair growth by rubbing animal fat onto their scalps or applying a ground up mixture of a dog's paw, a date pit, and an ass's hoof.

CLOTHING

Herodotus also noted the Egyptian custom regarding clothing: "They are especially strict about always wearing freshly laundered linen garments."[18] Linen was made from flax, a plant grown in abundance along the Nile. It had the advantage of being lightweight, which helped people stay comfortable in the hot sun. It also became stronger when it was wet, dried quickly, and was more decay resistant than most other natural fibers.

Clothing for men and women was simple. Men usually went barechested, wearing either loincloths around their waists or kilts with hems at knee level. In later years they added short-sleeved shirts and a kind of skirt that could reach their ankles. Women wore long, tube-like linen skirts. Wealthier women often added pleats and other ornamentation. Wealthier men and women also had ceremonial linen robes. Since the desert can get chilly in the winter, many also had woolen robes.

Clothing was even more basic for children. Youngsters of both sexes commonly were naked until they were about eight. At that point they began wearing clothes similar to their parents: kilts or loincloths for boys, simple dresses for girls. In addition, boys' heads were shaved, except for a tress of hair that might be braided and dangled over one ear. When they were about 10, they cut off the side lock and allowed their hair to grow evenly.

> **DID YOU KNOW?**
> The homes of the wealthy often had gardens, which included pools covered with water lilies and encircled by ornamental trees and flowers.

Most people went barefoot. For protection against sharp objects and for ceremonial occasions, they might put on sandals. There were two types: leather for the affluent and interwoven rushes for everyone else. Rush sandals wore out quickly, so they were reserved primarily for special occasions.

BEAUTY AND HYGIENE

As Herodotus's observation about clothing suggests, Egyptians placed a high value on cleanliness. This value extended to personal hygiene. An ancient text disparages a man by saying that "he washes himself but once a day."[19] The implication is that other, more socially acceptable people washed more often.

Frequent washing—which included cleaning the hands and face before and after meals—was just one element of maintaining a pleasing personal appearance. Another daily ritual involved cleaning the mouth with the mineral salt natron dissolved in water. Continual exposure to sun, wind, and dust made skin care especially important. Combining plant extracts with various types of animal fats produced ointments that kept skin soft and supple and helped to avoid wrinkles, something that concerned Egyptians as much as people today.

Perhaps the most distinctive aspect of ancient Egyptian portraits and statues is the doe-eyed look. Both men and women paid special attention to making their eyes stand out to make themselves especially attractive. They ground up minerals such as galena or malachite to form a black paste known as kohl. Using thin wooden or bone rods—or even their fingers—Egyptians applied kohl in thick lines onto their eyebrows and around their eyes.

To add to the effect of making up their eyes, Egyptians liked to grind red ochre into a powder and mix it with water, then dab it onto their cheeks and lips. They used henna to color their fingernails in shades of yellow and orange.

HAIR CARE

For Egyptians, the crowning glory of personal appearance—literally—was a full head of hair. "Human hair was of great importance in ancient Egypt," writes Egyptologist Joann Fletcher. "Rich or poor of both genders treated hair—their own or locks obtained elsewhere—as a highly pliable means of self-expression."[20] If they could afford to, Egyptians of both sexes wore wigs. There were several reasons for this. One was the prevalence of head lice. Cropping their hair or even shaving it eliminated that problem. Another was comfort. Wigs had a base of vegetable fibers that kept them from resting directly on the scalp, thereby making them slightly cooler than natural hair. A third was that wigs provided a quick way of proclaiming wealth and status. Elaborately arranged wigs indicated that the person was important, as they were very time-consuming and expensive to produce and maintain. Yet another reason was vanity. Graying hair and natural baldness were considered unattractive or even shameful, and wigs concealed those "faults."

Many people tried to "cure" gray hair by coloring it. One recipe called for boiling the blood of a black cat or a bull, blending it in oil,

The ancient Egyptians were attentive to their looks. A painted limestone statue of an Old Kingdom queen shows the kohl-lined eyes and brows and a type of wig popular with both men and women.

then adding magic incantations. Wig colors were not limited to the dark hair natural for Egyptians. Some were red or even blond.

Men also had to deal with facial hair. Because beards were not fashionable, Egyptian men of all social classes usually began their day by shaving. There was one exception. Beards were regarded as sacred to the gods, so kings—and sometimes queens—on ceremonial occasions would put on a narrow false beard that hooked around their ears and dangled as much as 1 foot (30cm) below their chins.

PHYSICAL ADORNMENTS

Smelling good was especially important to Egyptians. That could be difficult, as a hot climate doubtless generated a great deal of perspiration. Bathing in the Nile (or for the wealthy, at home) was one solution. Perfumes were another. Perfume production was a thriving industry. Scented minerals such as myrrh, fragrant plants like lotus, or even spices like cinnamon or cardamom were mixed with substances such as olive oil or sesame oil. Some of the most exotic perfume ingredients were said to have come from Punt, a semilegendary East African country noted for its special fragrances.

There can be little doubt of the effectiveness of the resulting products. When the god Amun-Ra visited a queen who was sleeping, "she waked at the fragrance of the god, which she smelled in the presence of his majesty," according to ancient records. "When he came before her, she rejoiced at the sight of his beauty, his love passed into her limbs, which the fragrance of the god flooded; all his odors were from Punt."[21] Such ravishing scents had similar effects on earthly couples.

These physical adornments were often accompanied by staggering amounts of ancient Egyptian bling. Egyptian jewelers were incredibly skilled. Working with primitive equipment, they produced earrings, necklaces, rings, bracelets, and brooches of breathtaking beauty. Using materials such as agates, beads, coral, jade, pearls, and shells, they created images of fish, flowers, gods and goddesses, geometric shapes, and much more.

A High Standard of Living

Taken together, the combination of a stable home life, comfortable houses, plentiful food, and personal adornment provided Egyptians with one of the highest standards of living in the ancient world. Because they were so well off, especially in comparison to people in other regions of the ancient world, they had no need or desire to move elsewhere and form new colonies. They were content to stay in their homes along the Nile and take full advantage of the river's bounty.

CHAPTER 2

Work and Play

One reason that Egyptian society lasted for so many years was the order and stability provided by the country's pyramidal social class structure. The primary difference among the various classes was the amount of wealth and power they had. Especially during the first half of the long duration of Egyptian civilization, a person would almost always remain in the class into which he or she had been born.

FARMING

The base of the pyramid, and by far the largest class, was the mass of common people consisting mainly of farmers. More than any other group, the rhythms of their life were dictated by the rise and fall of the Nile.

As the river began subsiding, timing became critical. If the farmers waited too long, the sun would bake the topsoil almost solid, making it nearly impossible to plow. So they would get up at dawn or even before, shave and wash, eat a simple breakfast, then hurry out into their fields while the ground was still damp, often with standing water in a few places. Hitching their plows to cattle, they began the hard work of turning over the still-waterlogged earth. When cattle were not available, the men took turns being hitched to the plow or used hoes to turn over the earth. As the gaps in the earth opened up, they scattered the precious seeds—wheat, barley, flax, and more—and covered them. To keep birds from gobbling up the newly sown seeds, farm animals were turned loose to tamp down the earth and bury the seeds more deeply.

Within a few months the crops were ready to be harvested. Farmers went through the fields of waving grain, using sickles with wooden handles and flint blades to shear off the heads. Women and children trailed behind them and picked up the precious heads of the grain. The stalks were gathered later as fodder for the farm animals.

The heads were taken to the threshing floor. Donkeys or cattle walked back and forth, their steps separating the grain from its protective husks. Women scooped up heaping handfuls of grain and husks and hurled them into the air. The wind whisked away the lightweight husks, while the heavier grain fell back at their feet.

Sometimes slaves worked in the fields alongside farmers and their families. Slaves ranked below farmers in the social system, though they

A peasant couple plow and plant a field in this scene from a wall painting found in a New Kingdom tomb. Plowing usually began soon after the Nile's flooding subsided.

formed a small proportion of the overall population and, in general, participated in the prosperity of Egyptian society. Most slaves were obtained through war and trade. They could not own property, but they could marry into the families that owned them or be adopted. Especially competent and enterprising slaves who impressed their masters might be granted their freedom. Many, if not most, slaves were eventually absorbed into Egyptian society.

THE RAW MATERIAL FOR LINEN

The procedure for harvesting flax, the source of the linen that nearly everyone wore, was slightly different than that for wheat. Flax was harvested early, typically while it was still blooming, because younger fibers were especially strong. Unlike wheat, it was pulled up by the roots, and the stalks were cooked and then allowed to partially rot. At this point they would be separated and eventually spun into thread. Wealthy individuals got the highest-quality thread, while farming families wore clothing made of more coarse threads.

> **DID YOU KNOW?**
> The Heb-Sed festival celebrated the thirtieth anniversary of a pharaoh's reign. To prove he was still potent, the pharaoh had to run around a field while carrying several ritual objects.

Many tombs of wealthy land-owners were lavishly illustrated with images of farming activities. Some have brief comments overhead, similar to balloons that convey dialogue in modern comic strips. Egyptologist Barbara Mertz believes that some of these comments might be more for show than a reflection of anyone's true feelings. "'Let's work,' a man exclaims enthusiastically in one image, and another declares that he will do even more than is expected of him 'for the noble,'" observes Mertz. "One is entitled to harbor a certain amount of skepticism about these admirable sentiments."[22]

Other inscriptions probably reflect actual conversations. An overseer urges his workers forward by saying, "I am telling you, men, the barley is ripe, and he who reaps well will get it."[23] Another illustrates that trash-talking is not a recent invention. "Even if you bring me 11009 (sheaves), I shall ripple them all,"[24] an older man boasts, referring to the procedure of pulling the flax plants through a comb-like device to separate the seeds from the rest of the plant so they can be planted the following year. "Hurry up and stop talking, bald-headed old fieldhand,"[25] retorts his younger companion.

During the months when their land was underwater, farmers could not afford to be idle. They became a huge labor force that helped build palaces, pyramids, temples, and other large projects.

The Middle Class

To function smoothly, a society as complex as that of ancient Egypt needed people working in many occupations—not just farmers. There was a thriving middle class consisting mainly of skilled tradespeople—metalworkers, jewelers, sculptors, potters, carpenters, glassmakers, and more. Because the people of ancient Egypt did not use money, craftspeople were paid in food, beer, housing, and other things they needed in their daily lives.

Typical of these skilled tradespeople were carpenters, who produced sturdy chairs, tables, stools, and other artifacts, despite having what today would be considered primitive tools and equipment. Most of their tools were made of copper—chisels, saws, axes, and so forth. They smoothed, or planed, the wood with lumps of stone. Drilling must have been especially arduous. Drills consisted of a bow with a length of twine fastened to each end; this spun a copper or bronze bit secured in a wooden shaft.

Primitive equipment was not the only limitation the tradespeople faced. As Mertz points out, carpenters "had reason to be proud of their skill, all the more so because of the materials they had to work with. Egypt is poor in large trees . . . carpenters had to learn to work, for the most part, with their scrubby native trees."[26]

The same limitations applied to those who made the jars, bowls, and bottles that contained the perfumes, eye makeup, powders, and other articles Egyptians deemed necessary to look their best. Given

HIEROGLYPHS

Few aspects of Egyptian life are more distinctive than the system of writing known as hieroglyphs, which dates back to at least 3250 BC. It was an elaborate form of picture writing, in which some hieroglyphs represented sounds, while others—the vast majority—depicted actual objects or ideas. For example, "to travel south" was a boat with its sail up to catch the predominant northerly wind. "To travel north" showed a boat with its sail down to move with the current. Often hieroglyphs were used in combinations. Scholars believe there were more than 700 individual hieroglyphs, and the system was deliberately kept complicated to help scribes maintain their position of power and authority. Hieroglyphs were more than a means of communication. Egyptians also considered their aesthetic value and regarded them as decorations. They were careful to arrange them in ordered lines to maintain a sense of balance.

the often difficult conditions under which they worked, it is remarkable that they were able to produce objects of such beauty.

A scribe named Dua-Khety provides insight into some of those working conditions. In a letter to his son, the scribe points out the benefits of following in his occupational footprints. Those who take up a trade, he explains, can expect many hardships and difficulties in their work. For example, "The weaver inside the weaving house is more wretched than a woman. His knees are drawn up against his belly. He cannot breathe the air. If he wastes a single day without weaving, he is beaten with 50 whip lashes. He has to give food to the doorkeeper to allow him to come out to the daylight."[27]

Conditions were not much better for other occupations. According to Dua-Khety, the fingers of a coppersmith "were like the claws of the crocodile, and he stank more than fish excrement," a potter "burrows in the field more than swine to bake his cooking vessels," and as an arrow maker cuts reeds by the river, "the gnats sting him and the sand fleas bite him."[28]

SCRIBES

No one knows if Dua-Khety persuaded his son to become a scribe. Accounts from other ancient Egyptians indicate a drawback of the scribe's profession that Dua-Khety almost certainly did not mention. According to Joann Fletcher, scribes were required to "love writing, shun dancing, cease hunting, befriend the scroll and palette."[29]

Scribes were very important; as the official keepers of all records, they collected taxes and coordinated massive building projects. Scholars dispute whether writing originated in Mesopotamia or in Egypt, but in Egypt it quickly took the form of a complex set of symbols called hieroglyphs. Egyptian kings were quick to recognize its importance. "Having been developed as an accounting tool, writing found an enthusiastic reception among bureaucratically minded Egyptians," writes Egyptologist Toby Wilkinson. "To be a scribe—to be able to read and write—was to have access to the levels of power."[30]

> **DID YOU KNOW?**
> Though Egyptians liked to dance, the available evidence suggests that men and women did not dance together.

Becoming a scribe guaranteed continual employment. The scribe's skills were of use in virtually every area of Egyptian society. It was also one of the relatively few jobs that allowed the practitioner to be upwardly mobile. With knowledge at a premium—according to estimates, just 1 or 2 percent of the population was literate—becoming a scribe could be a stepping-stone to a higher office. With skill, a good reputation, hard work, knowing the right people, and perhaps a little luck, a talented scribe could ascend almost to the top of Egyptian society.

GOVERNMENT OFFICIALS

As he rose into the upper class, the scribe would join high-ranking military officers, nobles, priests, and important government officials. With an estimated population of several million people, Egypt was perhaps the largest of all ancient societies. The country's unusual shape—covering several hundred miles from the southern border to the Mediterranean Sea while just a few miles in width—only increased the difficulties in governing. Even under ideal circumstances, a trip from one end to the other required several weeks. Accordingly, ancient Egypt was divided into 42 nomes, or provinces. Each was administered by a governor, who in essence ruled over his own little kingdom.

The highest official was the vizier, who was directly responsible to the king and whose authority extended over virtually every area of Egyptian life except religion. As Wilkinson notes, his duties included "hearing petitioners with a grievance against the authorities, presiding as chief judge in important cases, and receiving daily briefings from other government ministers. . . . As well as prime minister and first lord of the treasury, the vizier was effectively commissioner of police, minister for the armed forces, and interior minister as well."[31]

AT THE VERY TOP

The king was the capstone of the social pyramid. Today we refer to Egyptian kings as pharaohs. It is a term that means "great house." It originally referred to the huge palaces where the kings lived. During the New Kingdom period, beginning around 1539 BC, it was applied directly to the kings themselves. Pharaohs were regarded as partly divine. In case anyone missed that point, pharaohs customarily had five names, several of which referred directly to important gods.

To his subject people, the pharaoh's role was vital. Joyce Tyldesley notes:

> He, and he alone, could communicate with the fickle deities who controlled Egypt's destiny. . . . Without a pharaoh on the throne the gods could not receive the regular offerings of food,

drink, incense and prayer that they craved. . . . Deprived of their offerings the gods might grow dissatisfied; they might even be tempted to abandon Egypt, allowing chaos to overwhelm *maat*, or natural harmony.[32]

One indication of the importance of the pharaoh can be gauged by the fact that events were dated to the start of the reign of each new one. For example, the powerful pharaoh Ramesses II dated his rule by Year 1 of Ramesses II, Year 2 of Ramesses II, and so on, up to Year 67—making him the longest ruling of all the hundreds of pharaohs.

HUNTING AND OTHER SPORTS

From pharaoh on down to the lowliest farmer or slave, Egyptians worked hard. For years many classical scholars, such as Edith Hamilton, believed that a lifetime of hard labor was all that most Egyptians

Egypt's kings and nobles enjoyed hunting for waterfowl and other animals. Joined by his family, a member of the royal court hunts waterfowl in a marsh.

Military service was one of many occupational paths. Battles during the Old Kingdom consisted mostly of mobs of poorly trained men using elementary tactics. By the time of the Middle Kingdom, however, men were drafted on a regional basis to serve for a set period of time and undergo hard, often brutal training. Incentives encouraged them to remain as soldiers. They could share in booty from victorious campaigns and receive land when they retired. Sharp bronze swords and spears, bows and arrows accurate up to several hundred yards, body armor, and shields made of wood and leather all increased the likelihood that they could survive and enjoy those incentives.

While most men served in the infantry, the chariot corps—composed largely of wealthy Egyptians who could afford horses and the two-wheeled vehicles made of wood, leather, and wicker—was the elite arm of the Egyptian military. The driver steered the horses with one hand and with the other hand held a shield to protect his warrior, who was armed with a bow and arrow and a dozen or more javelins.

could look forward to. Hamilton, who greatly admired ancient Greece, wrote in 1930, "Wretched people, toiling people, do not play. Nothing like the Greek games is conceivable in Egypt. . . . The Egyptian did not play."[33]

The Egyptians were indeed "toiling people." But they probably were not as "wretched" as Hamilton claims they were. Egyptians at every level of society carved out leisure time. They took advantage of their sunny climate and enjoyed participating in sports and other recreational activities.

Among the nobility, hunting was popular. There was a wide variety of game, such as ducks and other waterfowl, wild cattle, gazelles, ostriches, and antelope. In open country, nobles would chase their quarry in their chariots, often accompanied by their dogs. Sometimes they hunted birds with falcons.

Pharaohs were especially attracted to hunting, often as a way of proving their strength and bravery. When he was about 12, Amenhotep III (who reigned from about 1390 BC to about 1353 BC) took part in a wild bull hunt and issued a commemorative coin that read: "The number the king took in hunting on this [first] day: 56 wild bulls. His Majesty waited four days to give his horses a rest. His Majesty appeared in the chariot [again]. The number of wild bulls he took in hunting: 40 wild bulls."[34] Later he issued another coin to boast that he had slain 110 lions during his first decade on the throne.

Some sports served as preparation for battle. Noblemen enjoyed chariot racing. Foot soldiers were likely to participate in sports such as boxing and wrestling.

A variety of non-war-related sports were also popular. These included foot racing, swimming in the Nile River, gymnastics, high jumping and long

jumping, a game similar to handball, and perhaps even very primitive versions of baseball and hockey. The proximity to the river gave rise to rowing races and boat competitions, in which each crew tried to knock its opponents into the water.

Many Egyptians had pets, with dogs and cats being especially popular. Both were also practical. Cats helped to keep homes free of mice and rats, while dogs were hunting companions and kept watch at night. According to Herodotus, Egyptians mourned the loss of their dogs even more than their cats: "All those who live in a household where a cat has died a natural death shave their eyebrows. For the death of a dog, however, they shave their entire body and head."[35] A number of households had more exotic pets, such as baboons and monkeys. Some pharaohs maintained extensive private zoos, which included lions and cheetahs.

GAMES

Egyptians enjoyed playing board games. One, called Hounds and Jackals, was similar to cribbage. Long, thin pegs with carved heads representing the two animals were moved from hole to hole on the playing board. Mehen was another popular game. The playing board was a circular surface that resembled a coiled snake. The pieces might be in the shape of crouching lions and bear the names of Egypt's early kings. The goal was to move them steadily toward the center of the board, where they could escape through the mouth of the snake. Senet, a third game, resembled modern-day backgammon and was played on a board with three rows of 10 squares each. Some of the squares were marked to indicate good or bad fortune. Each of two players had about seven pieces, which moved according to throws of dice-like objects called knucklebones. The object was to be the first to convey all the pieces to the finish.

Children of all social levels loved playing and had a wide variety of games and toys to choose from. Tomb inscriptions provide visual evidence of some of their favorite pastimes. In one game, two girls riding piggyback throw a ball back and forth. Since rubber was unknown, the ball was probably made of wood or chaff sewn inside a leather skin. In another game, two lines of boys play tug-of-war. But rather than pull on a rope, they hold each other by the wrists and pull mightily in opposite directions. In a third game, two boys sit facing each other with their arms stretched out. The other children apparently have to say when they are going to try to jump over an obstacle, and the two seated boys try to trip them.

Dolls and animal figures were also favorites at playtime. Both sexes had animal toys. Many toys had moving parts such as tails and legs or mouths that opened and closed by pulling on a string. Just as is the case in present times, girls played with dolls. It is likely that peasant dolls were simple, perhaps just a few sticks cobbled together. Girls from wealthier families had more sophisticated dolls, often with realistic human forms and moveable limbs and, in some cases, different sets of clothing.

FEASTS AND CELEBRATIONS

Egyptians enjoyed having a good time. Many tomb illustrations depict parties or other gatherings. The hosts of these parties dressed in their finest clothing and wore sparkling jewelry made of gold and other precious materials. Some guests arrived via chariots, while others reclined on litters borne by their servants. After making small talk, as a PBS special feature presentation notes, "It's soon time for dinner—a feast of geese and ducks, fresh fish, roasted ox, goat and gazelle. For dessert, there's grapes, melons, figs, dates, pistachio nuts and pomegranates, all served on golden plates. The wine flows freely and the guests love the music and dancers provided by their hosts."[36]

> **DID YOU KNOW?**
> Several viziers, such as Imhotep (who designed the Step Pyramid of King Djoser), achieved so much renown that eventually they were worshipped as gods.

The music came from early versions of modern-day harps, lutes, lyres, tambourines, drums, and flutes, either serving as background music or accompanying a singer. Musicians also provided the beat for dancers, who inspired their audience to clap and snap their fingers. The men in attendance probably enjoyed the servant girls, who passed among them with perfume and special treats, wearing little else besides a smile, a necklace, and the equivalent of a bikini bottom.

Herodotus notes one final custom that occurred before the party broke up and the guests staggered home:

At drinking parties of wealthy Egyptians, they always follow the end of their dinner by having a man carry around a corpse made of wood inside a coffin. The wooden corpse is crafted so as to be most realistic, both in the way it is painted and in the way it is carved, and it measures altogether one to three feet in length. As the man displays it before each of the guests, he says, "Look at this as you drink and enjoy yourself, for you will be like this when you are dead."[37]

While poor people obviously could not attend these lavish parties, they had plenty of opportunities to enjoy themselves in the numerous festivals accompanying the crowning of a new pharaoh, honoring one of the many gods, giving thanks for a successful harvest, and other notable civic celebrations. *National Geographic* magazine describes a typical festival:

Pilgrims arrived by the hundreds of thousands and set up camp. Music and dancing filled the processional route. Merchants sold food, drink, and souvenirs. Priests became salesmen, offering simply wrapped [animal] mummies as well as more elaborate ones for people who could spend more—or thought they should. With incense swirling all around, the faithful ended their journey by delivering their chosen mummy to the temple with a prayer.[38]

SOLID SOCIAL STRUCTURE

It seems clear that Egyptians were more than just "wretched." Children used their imaginations to play games that did not require much in the way of elaborate equipment or organized leagues. Their parents—no matter what their social level—could always look forward to the next party or public festival with a great deal of confidence.

Much of this confidence was due to the safety and sense of security that the social structure provided. The pharaoh and the bureaucracy that worked for him made Egypt one of the most orderly of all the ancient countries. People could go to sleep at night knowing that their world would be the same when they woke up the following morning.

CHAPTER 3

Community Life

From farmer to pharaoh, Egyptians of all social levels were impacted in their daily lives by several aspects unrelated to their homes and jobs. These aspects were all part of maat, the belief system that regulated Egyptian life and was a primary reason for the country's long-term stability.

LAW

Ancient Egypt had a well-developed system of laws. Though these laws were not written down, Egyptologists say that they were well understood among the population. Scribes kept detailed records, so judges had precedents they could use in deciding cases.

Unlike most other ancient societies, all Egyptians were considered equal under the law, regardless of occupation or wealth. They could even plead their own cases. This idea was emphasized in the Instructions of Rekhmire, a series of injunctions given to the incoming vizier Rekhmire by Pharaoh Thutmose III, who reigned from around 1479 BC to about 1425 BC. "Behold, when a petitioner comes . . . see to it that everything is done in accordance with law, that everything is done according to the custom thereof, giving to every man his right," said the pharaoh. "Forget not to judge justice. It is an abomination of the god to show partiality."[39]

This equality meant that women had many of the same rights as men. In particular, they could divorce their husbands, and they would not be ruined. They could even own property. As Barbara Mertz points out, "The importance of a woman's ability to own property can hardly be overstated. Financial independence is, and has always been, the foundation on which all other rights of women must be based, and it was a right not obtained by married women in England and America—those great democracies—until the late nineteenth century A.D."[40]

THE TALE OF THE ELOQUENT PEASANT

One of the best-known stories from ancient Egypt, *The Tale of the Eloquent Peasant*, displays this ideal of justice. The story begins when a peasant named Khun-Anup leaves home with several grain-laden donkeys. A minor official named Nemtynakht sees Khun-Anup approaching and schemes to rob him.

Because the road narrows between a barley field and a pond, Nemtynakht spreads a linen sheet across the road and orders the peasant to make sure his donkeys do not step on it. As the animals gingerly step around the sheet, one of them bends down and chomps a mouthful of barley. This "crime" enables Nemtynakht to confiscate the donkeys and their goods. For good measure he pummels Khun-Anup.

Instead of going back home, Khun-Anup appeals to Rensi, the high steward whom Nemtynakht serves. Somehow Khun-Anup has learned to speak eloquently, and the beauty of his language and the force of his argument are literally music to Rensi's ears. Rensi appears to ignore Khun-Anup even though he is in agreement with what the peasant has to say. That way he manages to get Khun-Anup to return so he can enjoy the beauty of his words. Eight more times, in fact.

Rensi also passes word of this remarkable peasant to the pharaoh, who is just as smitten with Khun-Anup's oratory. The pharaoh orders Rensi to detain Khun-Anup so every word can be recorded and to feed the peasant's family during his absence. In the end Khun-Anup wins over both the pharaoh and Rensi and gets his donkeys and his grain back. The pharaoh also orders Nemtynakht to surrender all his possessions to the peasant.

The moral of the story is clear. If a peasant at the base of the social pyramid can appeal for justice and win out over his social superiors, anyone can. As Mertz observes, "The argument of the peasant, and the events of the tale, pronounced the same conclusion—justice is the same for rich and poor alike. It is a conclusion that may startle us, coming at this time and this place."[41]

CRIME AND PUNISHMENT

No society has ever been free from lawbreakers, and Egypt was no exception. Most crimes were relatively minor. "They went to the granary, stole three great loaves and eight sabu-cakes of Rohusu berries," lamented a victim of petty theft. "They drew a bottle of beer which was cooling in water, while I was staying in my father's room. My Lord, let whatsoever has been stolen be given back to me."[42]

> **DID YOU KNOW?**
> Ancient Egyptian police used dogs and other animals in their work; one tomb illustration shows a monkey on a leash helping to apprehend a thief.

The plea might have been answered. Egypt had a rudimentary police force, with many of the same duties that characterize contemporary law enforcement officers. They gathered evidence, interrogated suspects (sometimes through torture), and tried to get confessions.

Egyptians considered criminal activity as opposed to maat, so perpetrators could face several different types of punishment. Beatings were common. So was confiscation of property. More severe punishments might involve being sent into exile or suffering the amputation of body parts, in particular hands, ears, tongues, and noses. Capital punishment was also a possibility—decapitation, impalement on a stake, being burned alive, being cast into the river to drown—but only the pharaoh could authorize executions. One of the worst possible punishments was to be executed and not given a proper burial, which the Egyptians regarded as absolutely essential to enter the afterlife.

MEDICINE

Egyptians were just as subject to injuries, illnesses, and diseases requiring medical attention as any other ancient culture. Since knowledge of disease-causing bacteria and germs was still many centuries away,

Physicians relied on established remedies as well as help from the gods in treating their patients. A twentieth-century lithograph depicts an Egyptian physician treating a patient for lockjaw, often an early symptom of tetanus.

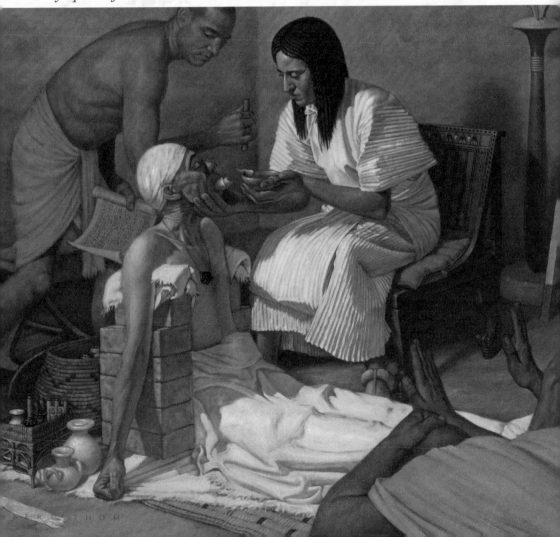

Egyptians thought that evil spirits caused many of their afflictions. They appealed to the gods for protection. Many people wore amulets with images of gods associated with healing. Not surprisingly, many early healers were priests.

Yet Egyptians did more than pray and cast spells. Several ancient documents reveal a high degree of medical skill that owes nothing to religion or magic. One of these is the Edwin Smith Papyrus, named after the American who purchased it in the nineteenth century. The document consists of 48 case studies of treatments that are at least 4,500 years old. For example, in treating a head wound, the Smith Papyrus says a physician should "palpate his wound, [though] he shudders greatly. You should cause him to lift his face. . . . Now if you find the cord of that man's mandible [lower jaw] is contracted, you should have made for him something hot until he is comfortable, so that his mouth opens. You should bind it with fat, honey, and lint."[43]

> **DID YOU KNOW?**
> Discovering the pulse was one of the great achievements of Egyptian medicine, though they had no way of accurately timing it.

The ancient Greek physician Hippocrates, who lived at roughly the same time as Herodotus, is generally regarded as the father of medicine. As the Smith Papyrus suggests, "paternity" may actually be nearly 2,000 years older. Says Jackie Campbell of the KNH Centre for Biomedical Egyptology at England's University of Manchester:

Our findings suggest that the ancient Egyptians were practicing a credible form of pharmacy and medicine much earlier. When we compared the ancient remedies against modern pharmaceutical protocols and standards, we found the prescriptions in the ancient documents not only compared with pharmaceutical preparations of today but that many of the remedies had therapeutic merit.[44]

MEASURING THE PASSAGE OF TIME

The Egyptians were the first people to base a calendar on the solar year. They divided the year into 12 months of 30 days each, with five more days for religious festivals that honored the birthday of major gods. This did not account for the extra one-fourth of a day (and a tiny fraction) of a genuine solar calendar, so occasionally a sixth day would be added to the festivals. The Egyptians also originated the 24-hour system of each day. Both night and day were divided into 12 equal parts, though the length of each hour varied according to the seasons. Daylight hours were longer in summer and shorter in winter, while night hours were longer in winter and shorter in summer.

PLENTY OF PRACTICAL KNOWLEDGE

Ancient Egyptian physicians were familiar with many useful remedies including those for constipation and various stomach problems. They knew how to get rid of tapeworms. They eased the suffering caused by rheumatism. They used plants such as acacia for coughs and aloe for skin irritations. "Many of the ancient remedies we discovered survived into the twentieth century and, indeed, some remain in use today, albeit that the active component is now produced synthetically," Campbell adds. "Other ingredients endure and acacia is still used in cough remedies while aloe forms a basis to soothe and heal skin conditions."[45]

Egyptian medicine frequently drew upon both magical ritual and practical knowledge. Physicians had many proven remedies they could employ to ease the suffering of their patients. At the same time, they were likely to appeal to the gods. Egyptologist Joann Fletcher quotes one example of this two-fold approach, which offers advice in dealing with burn victims: "Mix together the milk of a woman who has a son with gum and ram's hair. Apply it to the burn while saying, 'Your son Horus [the son of the goddess Isis] is burnt in the desert and needs water. But I have water in my mouth and the Nile between my thighs and I am here to extinguish the fire.'"[46]

Author/illustrator Mark Millmore quotes another two-fold treatment that illustrates the Egyptian emphasis on looking good: "If you are worried about wrinkles of the face try a ball of incense, wax, fresh oil, and cypress berries. Crush and rub down, put in new milk and apply it to the face for six days.... Take good heed to say the correct prayers with this remedy."[47]

Surprisingly, it appears that many Egyptian doctors were specialists. As Herodotus noted, "The art of medicine is divided so that each physician treats just one illness and no more. Doctors are everywhere, as there are specific physicians for the eyes, the head, the teeth, the abdomen, and still others for illnesses that are invisible."[48] This specialization could be carried to almost absurd lengths. According to J.H.D. Millar in the *Ulster Medical Journal*, "There was a keeper of the Pharaoh's right eye and also of his left eye. From hieroglyphics on a tomb we know that around 2500 B.C. a certain Doctor Iry was keeper of the Pharaoh's rectum."[49]

Egyptian physicians conducted operations using a variety of tools that included bone saws, drills, chisels, knives, suction cups, scalpels, and other devices. The agony of the victims, long before the days of anesthetics, must have been extreme.

DENTISTRY

Agony often extended to Egyptians' teeth. The emmer wheat that was the primary Egyptian grain had particularly strong husks. As a result, it required more threshing and grinding than other types of wheat. Since stones were used for grinding, tiny particles of stone chipped off and worked their way into the wheat. These chips turned up later in the baked bread, where they ground against the teeth of people eating the bread. The ever-present sand also worked its way into many meals, providing another source of friction. The result often was premature loss of tooth enamel.

That was just the start. According to the Discovery News website:

> Worn teeth, periodontal diseases, abscesses and cavities tormented the ancient Egyptians, according to the first systematic review of all studies performed on Egyptian mummies in the past 30 years [since 1979].
>
> After examining research of more than 3,000 mummies, anatomists and paleopathologists at the University of Zurich concluded that 18 percent of all mummies in case reports showed a nightmare array of dental diseases.[50]

Not surprisingly, the pharaoh and those close to him received much better care, with dedicated, highly skilled royal dentists at their beck and call. Everyone else had to take their chances with general practitioners, who may have had very limited experience with dentistry. Members of the nobility were more likely to need dental care, however, as their diet contained a higher proportion of cavity-causing sweets.

Egyptians believed that toothaches were caused by tooth worms that bored inside the teeth and crawled around. Sometimes a dentist would drill into the tooth and pull out a nerve, thinking it was a worm. The pain must have been intense during the operation, but once the nerve was gone, so was the toothache. Another remedy involved killing a mouse—an animal considered sacred to some gods—and holding it next to the tooth while the corpse was still warm.

And just as Egyptians used perfume to conceal body odor, many turned to some kind of breath sweetener to overcome the bad breath that often accompanied their less-than-ideal dental hygiene. One common sweetener was a combination of spices such as frankincense, myrrh, cinnamon, bark, and other fragrant plants. The mixture was

EDUCATION

Most Egyptians could not read or write, though virtually every child in Egypt received some form of education. Girls learned the household tasks their mothers performed, while boys received on-the-job training so they could practice the same occupation as their fathers. This method assured the continuity of vital skills and helped to preserve social order.

Children from wealthy families had a more formal education. Boys started with learning how to read and write, adding subjects like mathematics and literature as they grew older. In most cases learning was accomplished by copying. Teachers had little patience with slackers who were bored by writing the same thing over and over. According to an inscription, "A boy's ear is on his back—he listens when he is beaten." Some well-to-girls learned various forms of performing arts, such as singing and dancing.

Quoted in Mark Millmore, *Imagining Egypt: A Living Portrait of the Time of the Pharaohs.* New York: Black Dog & Leventhal, 2007, p. 131.

boiled with honey, then shaped into small pellets that were chewed or sucked like modern-day hard candy.

TAXES

Some Egyptians were fortunate enough to escape the need for medical care. But very few could escape being taxed. From the very beginning of Egyptian civilization, a system of taxation was vital to its stability. Because Egypt did not have a monetary system, taxes were usually paid in crops or livestock. The annual or biennial cattle count was an Egyptian institution. A famous wooden model found in a grave depicts a scribe named Meketre and his assistants sitting in a shaded pavilion while a wealthy man drives his cattle past him so they can be tallied.

Farmers seem to have been the most consistently taxed members of Egyptian society, as well as paying the highest rates. It was not hard to determine what they owed. The boundaries of each farmer's field were clearly marked, and therefore the amount due could easily be calculated: the larger the field, the higher the amount of grain the farmer had to give to the tax collectors. The rate could vary from year to year, depending on the level of Nile flooding.

Sometimes the farmer did not have enough grain to pay his entire tax bill. If that were the case, punishment was prompt and painful. "He [the farmer] is beaten hard," according to Mertz. "He is tied up and thrown into a pool. He is ducked and thoroughly soaked, and his wife is tied up in his presence."[51]

The treasury—the body charged with collecting taxes—was the most important branch of the pharaoh's government. Taxes were used in several ways. Some items were used to add even more income. For example, government-made linen from flax collected as taxes could be traded—often in other countries—for products the Egyptians could use. Some, especially grain, were stored as emergency rations in case of a bad harvest caused by abnormal flood patterns. And part went to the country's vast public works programs.

PUBLIC WORKS

During the flood season when farmers could not go into the fields, they often participated in public works projects, such as the building of pyramids, other funeral monuments, religious temples, and palaces. From the pharaoh's point of view, this work was absolutely essential. As Toby Wilkinson notes, "The royal tomb was designed to enable the king to continue presiding at royal ceremonies for all eternity. As such, the tomb was the essential guarantor of kingship and, from the rise of ancient Egypt until the demise of the pharaohs, the most important construction project of each reign."[52]

For many years, there was a popular misconception that these structures were built by slaves. More recent research has shown that the work was conducted by men who were paid for their work. As noted Egyptian archaeologist Zahi Hawass notes:

> There were permanent workmen who were working for the king. They were paid by the king. These are the technicians who cut the stones, and there are workmen who move the stones and they come and work in rotation. At the same time there are the people who live near the Pyramids that don't need to live at the Pyramids. They come by early in the morning and they work 14 hours, from sunrise to sunset.[53]

PALACES

Other major building projects were the vast, sprawling palaces where the pharaohs lived and ruled their kingdoms. The palace of Amenhotep III, for example, appears to have been the largest of all the palaces and covered well over 300,000 square feet (27,870 sq. m)—the size of 4 football fields.

Like other Egyptian residences, the palace was constructed primarily of mud bricks. With a work force that numbered in the thousands, however, it was far more elaborate than domiciles of other Egyptians. It was centered around a large apartment for the pharaoh that included a bedroom and private reception hall. It also had quarters for his children, audience halls, a library, storerooms, courtyards, accommodations for hundreds of servants, and gardens. Separate buildings housed his primary wife and provided

DID YOU KNOW?
The Nile's inundation helped in the construction of temples and palaces. Building materials and heavy stones could be loaded onto boats and carried to the site rather than being dragged.

The scribe Meketre and his assistants inspect and tally livestock from the comfort of a shaded pavilion, as depicted by a painted wooden model discovered in a Middle Kingdom–era tomb. The cattle count was essential for determining taxes owed to the government.

living and office space for his officials. The complex contained so many glass vessels that a factory had to be erected on-site to keep up with the demand. In addition to the various structures, workers dug a human-made lake and a canal linking the palace to the Nile River, where they added a mammoth artificial harbor.

As the palace walls began to rise, another set of workers—artists and painters—swarmed over the edifice. A few remaining fragments of plastered wall paintings provide a hint of the sumptuous decorations that once adorned the palace: portraits, scenes of life along the Nile, elaborate geometric patterns. To Mertz, these workers provided the true glory of the palace. "Floors, ceilings, and walls were painted in brilliant colors. . . . No greater contrast to the general view of Egyptian architecture—grim, gray, and monolithic—could possibly be imagined than these palaces, aglow with color and alive with the fluttering of birds' wings."[54]

Work on the palace of Amenhotep III apparently began in the early fourteenth century BC and took at least 20 years to complete. It quickly fell into disuse as his son and successor, Akhenaten, moved the capital to a new site—thereby requiring yet another massive building project.

IRRIGATION

Though pyramids and palaces were important symbolic public works projects, the most practical project was the system of irrigation because it was necessary to ensure a steady supply of water for crops. Because there was so little rainfall in Egypt, people were obsessive about water, feeling that literally every drop was vital to their survival and could not go to waste. Accordingly, water management through the irrigation system consumed huge amounts of time during the period between planting and harvesting.

DID YOU KNOW?
Many irrigation canals had an added benefit: catfish. It is likely that as floodwaters receded, the fish laid their eggs in the mud, and they hatched during the next inundation.

The irrigation system took advantage of yet another gift of the Nile. The highest land was located next to the river, with a gentle slope to the edges of the floodplain. "This made the valley especially suitable for irrigation, both by the natural floodwaters and by artificial means, since water would automatically come to rest, and remain longest, in the fields farthest from the riverbank—potentially the very areas most prone to drought," writes Wilkinson. "Moreover, the long, narrow floodplain naturally divides into a series of flood basins, each compact enough to be managed and cultivated with relative ease by the local population."[55]

As the Nile receded, considerable amounts of floodwater were captured through an elaborate system of dams and dikes that kept the water from flowing back into the river. Farmers distributed water through the growing season by an even more elaborate system of irrigation canals. Often they had to raise water manually from the ponds in which it was kept by lowering a bucket on a rope into the water. Then it was raised, hand over hand, and emptied into larger jugs. Two jugs fit into a yoke, which was balanced across a person's shoulders and carried to the point where they were needed.

Two devices helped with the otherwise backbreaking labor of raising water and emptying it into the canals. One was the *tanbour*, also known as an Archimedes' screw. It was a piece of wood in the shape of a screw inside a tight-fitting cylinder, with one end immersed in the Nile, a canal, or a well. As the screw was rotated, the water spiraled upward through the cylinder and eventually spilled over into a bucket or another canal. The other device was the *shaduf*, a long beam attached to a vertical pole. The beam had a weight on one end and a bucket on the other. The weight reduced the strain of lifting the filled bucket. Both are still in use today.

DID YOU KNOW?
A device called a Nilometer measured the height of the river at Egypt's southern border and provided an early indication of the height of the coming inundation.

ORDER AND STABILITY

One key element in the durability of Egypt was that water regulation appears to have been done primarily at the local level, rather than by the central government. As a result, dynastic disruption and external conquests had little effect on the ability of farmers to continue growing their crops, thereby helping to maintain the order and stability of daily life. This stability was also helped by the equality of all people before the law. This equality contributed to their willingness to embark on the vast public works we still regard with awe and that continue to make ancient Egypt so fascinating.

CHAPTER 4

Religion and the Afterlife

Religion was an essential element of everyday life in Egypt, perhaps more so than in any other ancient culture. This was the impression formed by Herodotus, at least. "Of all peoples, they [the Egyptians] are the most exceedingly pious,"[56] he said.

A LAND WITH MANY GODS

The Egyptians had hundreds of deities, which literally came in all shapes and sizes. Some resembled humans, whereas others embodied the Egyptian belief that certain animals had magical properties. Those gods might have an animal head on a human body or a form that was entirely animal—sometimes even a combination of two or more animals.

No matter what form divine beings took, they seemed to be tolerant of their worshippers, and vice versa. As Barbara Mertz observes:

They [the gods] lacked the nasty habits of some other deities, who thrived on incinerated babies and dripping human hearts or required the complete annihilation of people who held different opinions on religious matters.... If a foreigner could not find some Egyptian god or other to worship, he was very hard to please; but even in that case, the Egyptians allowed him to worship his own god, or adopted it themselves.[57]

One result of this tolerance was a variety of different myths to describe similar themes, such as the creation of the world. All of these variations were regarded as being equally valid. Another result of Egyptian tolerance in religious matters was the vast number and variety of gods. Originally, each town had its own god. As Egypt became more unified, these gods were absorbed into a larger religious structure that contained an ever-increasing number of divinities. There always seemed to be room for one more.

It was to everyone's benefit to ensure the constant blessings of these gods, which Egyptians felt influenced every act of daily life. Humans, they believed, owed their very existence to divine beings, and therefore these beings deserved continuous devotion and praise. Daily rituals took on a great deal of importance.

Many gods emerged from the observation of important natural phenomena. Obeying a genetic impulse far older than human civilization, crocodiles buried their eggs each year above what later would become the high-water mark of the flooding Nile River. In a civilization for which this information was vital, "Crocodiles were magical because they had that ability to foretell,"[58] according to noted Egyptologist Salima Ikram.

Eventually, crocodiles became associated with a water fertility god named Sobek, depicted either as a crocodile or a man's body with a crocodile's head. People, especially those who spent considerable amounts of time by the Nile, prayed to Sobek to protect them—from crocodiles. A shrine containing captive crocodiles was established at Kom Ombo in southern Egypt, one of the first places where the rising river could be observed. Provided with a steady diet of meat, the reptiles often became tame and were buried with honors when they died.

THE NILE SHAPES BELIEFS

The origins of Sobek are yet another example of the importance of the Nile River to the ancient Egyptians. The river affected not just their physical landscape, but also the way they thought about themselves and the world around them. One of their primary beliefs was maat, the state of equilibrium, or a balance between opposites. "This belief in the coexistence of opposites was characteristic of the ancient Egyptian mind-set, and was deeply rooted in their distinctive geographical situation," notes Toby Wilkinson. "This view was reflected in the contrast between the arid desert and the fertile floodplain, and in the river itself, for the Nile could both create life and destroy it."[59]

Maintaining maat and staving off chaos was therefore of vital importance to the Egyptians. As Joann Fletcher notes, "The Egyptians did all in their power to regulate and control this cosmic equilibrium, which they believed could be maintained only with the co-operation of their numerous gods and goddesses. In a reciprocal arrangement, the deities kept the universe in order while their vital role was acknowledged by daily acts of worship and a constant flow of offerings which replenished their powers."[60]

TWO TYPES OF RELIGION

There were actually two types of religion: the official state religion and a more personal, household version. The official state religion dealt with the divinity of the pharaoh and the proper way to run the government. It included the major gods such as Thoth, the moon god and god of writing and counting; Hathor, the goddess of love; Ra, the sun god; and Amun, a creator god. Often the last two were combined as Amun-Ra, an especially powerful god.

These major gods had temples dedicated to their worship. Only the priests who served the god and the pharaoh were allowed inside. At designated times during the year, public festivals honoring each god provided a welcome break in the routine of daily life and were also a source of free food and beer distributed to the general population.

In the mythology of the ancient Egyptians, the god Osiris (pictured in an image from the New Kingdom era) was Egypt's first pharaoh. For a time, after his death, he ruled the underworld.

A central myth of this official religion accounted for the divinity of the pharaoh. According to the myth, the god Osiris was the first pharaoh of Egypt, and he was married to his sister Isis. When he brought civilization and all its benefits to Egypt, his brother Seth was jealous. So he murdered Osiris, hacked him up into little pieces, and scattered them along the Nile. Isis gathered up the pieces, put them back together, and brought Osiris back to life. She promptly became pregnant with their son, Horus.

> **DID YOU KNOW?**
> The costliest mummies included individually wrapped toes—sometimes in gold leaf—to make sure they would not fall off.

Horus avenged his father's slaying, defeating Seth in a pitched battle and becoming king. Osiris took up a new position as king of the underworld. Eventually, Horus died, replacing his father as underworld king. At the same time, his son became the new Horus.

According to Egyptian religion, the pharaoh was identified with Horus. First he was the living king—thereby asserting his divinity—and then became Osiris when he died. It was a sign to the Egyptian people that the pharaoh was able to triumph over death—and that he was the earthly representative of the gods and goddesses.

RELIGION IN THE HOME

The other form of Egyptian religion might be called "household" religion. It probably had a more direct effect on the daily lives of the people than the official version. Houses, no matter how large or how small, contained a shrine to one or more of the gods. Part of the daily ritual of the inhabitants was to lay out a daily offering, no matter how modest.

These household shrines were centered around a small statue of a god. The most common were the gods Bes and Taweret, both of whom were associated with protecting women—particularly leading up to and during childbirth—and children. In the homes of those who could afford beds, images of one or the other were often carved into

ANIMAL MUMMIES

People were not the only living creatures to receive careful burial. When a dog named Abuwtiyuw that belonged to one of the early pharaohs died, according to the animal's tomb inscription, "His Majesty ordered that he be buried, that he be given a coffin from the royal treasury, fine linen in great quantity, incense. His Majesty gave perfumed ointment and [ordered] that a tomb be built for him by the gang of masons."

Abuwtiyuw was hardly exceptional. Because of Egyptians' belief in the afterlife, pets were often buried with their owners so they could romp and play together for eternity. Other animals were buried to provide plentiful food. And there is considerable evidence that the burial process for animals was as careful as it was for humans. "Millions of animal mummies are known to exist, and there is some debate whether they were treated with the same sort of reverence and sophistication as human mummies," says Richard Evershed, coauthor of a recent study about Egyptian burial practices. "We found pretty much exactly the same materials were used on both."

Quoted in Ancient Egypt, "Farmed and Domesticated Animals," September 2010. www.reshafim.org.il/ad.

Quoted in James Owens, "Egyptian Animals Were Mummified Same Way as Humans," *National Geographic News*, September 15, 2004. http://news.nationalgeographic.com.

headrests to guard against the stealthy entry of snakes, scorpions, and other dangers of the night.

In addition to daily offerings, another important way of gaining favor from the gods was by wearing amulets. These were small pieces of jewelry that came in a vast array of shapes and sizes and were often worn as necklaces. The most popular had miniature images of a god or of symbols associated with a particular god. Egyptians did not consider themselves fully dressed for the day's activities until they put on their amulets.

IMPORTANCE OF THE AFTERLIFE

The influence of religion did not stop with a person's death. A key element in Egyptian thought was a strong belief in an afterlife. Making it to the afterlife was not automatic; rather, living correctly was essential to enter the next world. Not long after people died, the ancient Egyptians believed, they would appear before Osiris, the god of the underworld, and a panel of 42 judges known as the Assessors. Before this group, the deceased would try to show that he or she had led an ethical life. Then came the weighing of the heart. Anubis, the jackal-headed god of cemeteries and embalming, placed the heart on a delicate scale. The heart had to be in exact balance with the feather of truth that belonged to the goddess Maat. If it was, the person moved on and joined Osiris in the afterlife as the god Thoth recorded the happy event.

> **DID YOU KNOW?**
> Egyptian burials took place on the west side of the Nile because the sun sets in the west.

However, if the weight of sin was too heavy, the heart would be devoured by Ammut, a frightening composite beast that combined deadly anatomical features of the Egyptians' three worst natural enemies: the rows of razor-sharp teeth in a crocodile's head, the powerful paws and forequarters of a lion, and the hindquarters of a hippopotamus. Because a person's spirit was believed to reside in the heart, its disappearance denied them the opportunity to proceed to the afterlife.

To prevent such a horrid fate, the Egyptians developed a system of chants, prayers, and other rituals known as the Book of the Dead. It ensured that the deceased would know what to say in the presence of Osiris and other gods who judged them. One vital part of the Book of the Dead consisted of a Negative Confession, a detailed list of literally dozens of sins that the newly deceased person maintained he or she had not committed during his or her lifetime. "I have not committed crimes against people," "I have not mistreated cattle," "I have not killed or ordered anyone to kill," and "I have not taken milk from children's mouths"[61] were some examples.

EVEN IN DEATH, LOOKS MATTERED

Detailed knowledge of the contents in the Book of the Dead was not enough. The Egyptian emphasis on looking and smelling good did not end with death. At the Judgment of the Dead, it was essential to follow certain rules of dress and makeup in order to make the right impression. According to the Book of the Dead, "A man says this speech [the Negative Confession] when he is pure, clean, dressed in fresh clothes, shod in white sandals, painted with eye-paint, anointed with the finest oil of myrrh."[62]

While the spirit of the dead person was undergoing this ritual, his or her body was hardly being neglected. Once the spirit passed into the afterlife, it needed the body for its continued survival. Preserving the body in the best possible condition was regarded as absolutely vital. It was also important that the dead be provided with artifacts they would need in the afterlife; even modest burials included food, furniture, cosmetics, and other items of daily life. The more important and more prosperous the individual, the more items would be included in the tomb.

Originally, Egyptians were buried in pits dug into the hot desert sand. The sand quickly absorbed the dead person's body fluids, producing dried-out corpses that bore at least a passing resemblance to what they had looked like while they were still alive.

The first attempts to improve on nature appear to have come several centuries before the start of dynastic rule, which is traditionally dated at about 2950 BC. During this time, the Egyptians began burying their dead in stone tombs. They soon discovered that without continual exposure to sand and intense heat, the bodies quickly decomposed.

MUMMIFICATION

That discovery cleared the way for the process of mummification, which became perfected by about 2500 BC. Scholars believe that *mummy* comes from the Persian word *mummiya*, meaning "bitumen" and describing the blackened state of ancient Egyptian bodies. No one knows how many people were mummified during the course of Egyptian history. While pharaoh mummies are the best known, according to some estimates the number may have been 70 million or even higher.

Mummification began with a period of mourning. Then the actual process began. There were several options, depending on the ability of the family to pay. The most expensive, as well as the best-known, began with removing the internal organs. First out was the brain, which was often removed with an iron hook. It came out in several chunks and was disposed of. In that era the brain's function was unknown. There is evidence that Egyptians believed that people thought with their hearts. This was not an unreasonable belief; it seemed obvious that in times of excitement, the heart beat faster, while the brain remained largely immobile.

> **DID YOU KNOW?**
> Priests adhered to the highest standards of cleanliness. They bathed frequently and wore gowns made of the finest linen.

Then an incision was made in the chest cavity, and most of the contents were removed. Four organs—stomach, intestines, lungs, and liver—were placed in separate containers called canopic jars. Each jar had an image of one of the sons of the god Horus on the stopper, and

Tomb Robbers

Nearly all Egyptians considered tombs and their contents to be sacred and untouchable. Breaking into those tombs and stealing the contents supposedly deprived dead people of things they would need in the afterlife, so tomb robbers who were caught received harsh punishment, sometimes even execution. That threat did not deter thieves, who sometimes were the same men who had helped to construct the tombs. They hacked their way into the tombs in spite of elaborate security measures designed by the architects. These measures included resting heavy slabs of rock against the doors and completely filling chambers leading to the entrance with tons of sand or stones.

No matter what the builders did to deter them, the thieves always seemed to find a way to break in. Eventually, nearly every tomb was looted of its priceless treasures. That is why archaeologists were so excited by the discovery of the tomb of the pharaoh Tutankhamun in 1922. King Tut, as he is commonly known, died when he was a teenager and was one of Egypt's least important rulers. Somehow tomb robbers had not discovered his final resting place. Its spectacular contents had remained untouched for thousands of years.

the jars would be reunited with the mummy in the tomb. Because of the importance of the heart and its necessity in the afterlife, it remained inside the body.

For families with less money, there was a cheaper method of organ removal. It involved injecting a solution resembling modern-day turpentine through the anus. Eventually, the solution would dissolve the internal organs and the mixture would be drained.

When the extractions were complete, fragrant substances were placed inside the cavity and it was sewn up. For the next 40 to 70 days, the body was covered with natron salts, which had a particular capacity for absorbing water.

Once this procedure was completed, the remains were little more than skin and bones. They weighed just a fraction of the body's original weight, perhaps 10 to 15 pounds (4.5kg to 6.8kg) for an average-sized Egyptian. Then the embalmer would literally stuff the body—using materials such as sawdust, ashes, salt, and similar substances—so that it returned to a semblance of its original shape. After that, makeup was applied to the face to make it as pleasing as possible.

Now the wrapping process began. The corpse was laid on a table and swaddled in layer after layer—as many as 20, according to some sources—of strips of linen. Amulets might be inserted between the layers—each one accompanied by a priest reading a spell—and at least twice the bandages were coated with warm resin. Finally the mummy took on the familiar columnar shape and was covered with a shroud with the image of Osiris inked in front. It was ready to be placed into a coffin and taken to the burial site. The ritual ended when the priest overseeing the whole process said, "You are alive; you are alive forever. Behold, you are young again and forever."[63]

DESTRUCTION OF MUMMIES

"Forever" became "short-lived" as many, if not most, of the mummies that had been so painstakingly prepared were eventually destroyed. Some were ripped apart as tomb robbers looked for jewels wrapped inside the layers of linen. Some were eliminated by religious extremists who regarded them as examples of paganism. For many years, ground-up mummies were used as medicine to cure a variety of maladies. For example, King Francis I of France (who reigned from 1515 to 1547), carried a pouch of ground-up mummy around his waist and swallowed some of the grains every day in the belief it would shield him

These ancient bronze surgical knives might have been used to remove the brain and internal organs during the mummification process. The brain, whose function was unknown at the time, was pulled out in pieces and discarded.

from potential assassins. Mummies could even be used as a source of heat. As Ikram explains, "There are 19th-century accounts of travelers who say, 'Oh, it's unseasonably cold and we've run out of wood, so we have to throw a mummy on the fire.'"[64]

Perhaps the most bizarre means of destruction occurred during the Victorian era in England in the nineteenth century. According to Ikram, "Mummies were considered very Gothic. And in the Victorian era, when anything neo-Gothic was cool, unwrapping mummies became very stylish. So people would bring back or buy mummies from Egypt and have unwrapping parties. We have invitations saying, 'Come to Lord Longsberry's at 2 p.m., Piccadilly, for the unwrapping of a mummy from Thebes. Champagne and canapés to follow.'"[65]

Many people could not afford mummification. They would be buried in the sand and covered with rocks. The dry desert air would perform natural mummification—so well, in fact, that some corpses are better preserved than the mummies of the ancient Egypt's wealthiest citizens.

BIG BUSINESS

Building and furnishing funerary monuments was big business, almost certainly the largest single industry in ancient Egypt. The embalmers—who probably passed down their trade secrets from generation to generation—were just one part of the business. They headed up workshops that employed a wide variety of personnel. The lowest ranking were the cutters who actually made the incisions into the body. Their work was regarded as unclean because of the belief that they could be in direct contact with evil spirits. The shop also needed workers to build coffins. And one or more scribes had to keep track of all the details.

The people directly involved in embalming were supported by a vast infrastructure. For starters, mummies needed copious amounts of linen. The mummy of one pharaoh contained about 9,000 square feet (836 sq. m) of linen—which would cover the entire playing field of a Major League Baseball stadium. The vast amounts of cloth required meant growing a lot of flax and then turning it into linen.

Much of the production from craftspeople went directly from their shops to the tomb. Since Egyptians expected the same standard of living in the afterlife, anything they could use while alive would also be used after death. Then there was the process of actually building the tomb where the mummy would be interred. That entailed still more workers, up to thousands in the case of pharaohs.

THE EGYPTIAN VIEW OF LIFE AND DEATH

To some people, the Egyptian emphasis on death and the afterlife became the basis for a negative evaluation of the entire civilization. For example, Edith Hamilton wrote in *The Greek Way*, originally published in 1930, "To the Egyptian the enduring world of reality was not the one he walked in along the paths of every-day life but the one he should presently go to by the way of death.... The lives and fortunes of all were completely dependent upon the whims of a monarch whose only law was his own wish.... Only in the world of the dead could there be found security and peace and pleasure."[66]

One of the twentieth century's most noted Egyptologists, Pierre Montet, took issue with this negative thinking. He admired his subjects' way of life, and his studies resulted in an almost opposite conclusion. "We can no longer accept the picture of the Egyptians as a horde of slaves impotent before the whims of a merciless Pharaoh," he wrote not long after Hamilton. "For the ordinary Egyptian, the good moments of life outnumbered the bad."[67]

Most modern scholars seem to have adopted this more positive opinion. They point out that Egyptians were not so preoccupied with death itself as they were with the means of overcoming it. Thus, nearly after a century after Hamilton, Jason Thompson reiterated the favorable view of ancient Egyptian culture. "The inordinate amount of attention that the ancient Egyptians devoted to death and the afterlife was not an expression of morbidity," he wrote. "Quite the contrary. They enjoyed life and wanted to experience it for all time."[68]

The last word on the subject might actually be among the first. Writing well over 4,000 years ago—long before Hamilton, Montet, Thompson, or the many other people who have commented on Egyptian life—Ptahhotep offered some advice that sounds as if it could have been written today:

> Follow your heart as long as you live...
> Don't waste time on daily cares
> Beyond providing for your household;
> When wealth has come, follow your heart,
> Wealth does no good if one is glum![69]

This sentiment was echoed on a number of Egyptian tombs, which carried the equivalent of the popular motto "carpe diem," or "seize the day." With an average life expectancy of about 40, the ancient Egyptians knew their days on earth were numbered. They wanted to enjoy them and to look forward to an even better afterlife.

The primary result of this belief system was a stable, long-lasting faith that endured for more than three millennia with hardly any changes and thereby provided the underpinning of the entire civilization. In a sense, therefore, Egyptians have indeed cheated death. Their civilization continues to attracts scholars and tourists and exerts a fascination and level of interest that few others can match.

SOURCE NOTES

INTRODUCTION: THE GIFT OF THE NILE

1. Herodotus, *The Landmark Herodotus: The Histories*, ed. Robert B. Strassler, trans. Andrea L. Purvis. New York: Pantheon, 2007, p. 156.
2. Herodotus, *Histories*, p. 118.
3. Jason Thompson, *A History of Egypt: From Earliest Times to the Present*. New York: Anchor, 2008, p. 5.
4. Quoted in Joyce Tyldesley, *The Pharaohs*. London: Quercus, 2009, p. 15.
5. Tyldesley, *The Pharaohs*, p. 6.
6. Thompson, *History of Egypt*, p. 38.

CHAPTER ONE: HOME AND FAMILY LIFE

7. Herodotus, *Histories*, p. 133.
8. John Ray, *Reflections of Osiris: Lives from Ancient Egypt*. New York: Oxford University Press, 2002.
9. Quoted in Tour Egypt, "The Life of Ancient Egyptians: Marriage and the Standing of Women." www.touregypt.net.
10. Quoted in Ancient Egypt, "Aspects of Daily Life," February 2010. www.reshafim.org.il/ad.
11. Quoted in Tour Egypt, "The Life of Ancient Egyptians."
12. Ilene Springer, "The Egyptian Bride," Tour Egypt. www.touregypt.net.
13. Quoted in Humanistic Texts, "Ptahhotep," 1999. www.humanistictexts.org.
14. Quoted in K.C. Hanson's Collection of Greek Documents, "Marriage Contract from Elephantine, Egypt," May 1, 2007. www.kchanson.com.
15. Quoted in Ancient Egypt, "Man and Woman," February 2010. www.reshafim.org.il/ad.

16. Horst Dornbusch, "Egyptian Beer for the Living, the Dead . . . and the Gods," *BeerAdvocate*, February 28, 2005. http://beeradvocate.com.

17. Herodotus, *Histories*, p. 155.

18. Herodotus, *Histories*, p. 134.

19. Quoted in Ancient Egypt, "The Instruction of Dua-Khety," September 2004. www.reshafim.org.il/ad.

20. Quoted in Ilene Springer, "Great Hair Days in Ancient Egypt," Tour Egypt. www.touregypt.net.

21. Quoted in Ancient Egypt, "Personal Hygiene and Cosmetics," November 2009. www.reshafim.org.il/ad.

Chapter Two: Work and Play

22. Barbara Mertz, *Red Land, Black Land: Daily Life in Ancient Egypt*. New York: William Morrow, 2009, p. 298.

23. Quoted in Thompson, *A History of Egypt*, p. 37.

24. Quoted in Ancient Egypt, "Flax," February 2007. www.reshafim.org.il/ad.

25. Quoted in Ancient Egypt, "Flax."

26. Mertz, *Red Land, Black Land*, p. 101.

27. Quoted in Ancient Egypt, "The Instruction of Dua-Khety."

28. Quoted in Ancient Egypt, "The Instruction of Dua-Khety."

29. Joann Fletcher, *The Egyptian Book of Living and Dying*. London: Duncan Baird, 2009, p. 104.

30. Toby Wilkinson, *The Rise and Fall of Ancient Egypt*. New York: Random House, 2010, p. 41.

31. Wilkinson, *The Rise and Fall of Ancient Egypt*, pp. 226–227.

32. Tyldesley, *Pharaohs*, p. 6.

33. Edith Hamilton, *The Greek Way*. New York: Norton, 1993, p. 25.

34. Quoted in Wilkinson, *The Rise and Fall of Ancient Egypt*, p. 241.

35. Herodotus, *Histories*, p. 146.

36. *Egypt's Golden Empire*, "A Day in the Life: Nobleman," PBS.org. www.pbs.org.

37. Herodotus, *Histories*, p. 151.

38. A.R. Williams, "Animal Mummies," *National Geographic*, November 2009. http://ngm.nationalgeographic.com.

CHAPTER THREE: COMMUNITY LIFE

39. Quoted in Don Ferruggia's Web Pages, "Instructions of Rekhmire." www.donf.com.
40. Mertz, *Red Land, Black Land*, p. 64
41. Barbara Mertz, *Temples, Tombs and Hieroglyphs*. New York: William Morrow, 2007, p. 125.
42. Quoted in Mark Millmore, *Imagining Egypt: A Living Portrait of the Time of the Pharaohs*. New York: Black Dog & Leventhal, 2007, p. 132.
43. Quoted in Mertz, *Red Land, Black Land*, pp. 252–253.
44. Quoted in ScienceDaily, "Egyptians, Not Greeks Were True Fathers of Medicine," May 9, 2007. www.sciencedaily.com.
45. Quoted in ScienceDaily, "Egyptians, Not Greeks Were True Fathers of Medicine."
46. Quoted in Fletcher, *The Egyptian Book of Living and Dying*, p. 113.
47. Quoted in Millmore, *Imagining Egypt*, p. 142.
48. Herodotus, *Histories*, p. 152.
49. J.H.D Millar, "The Medical Library: Annual Oration at the Opening of the 1975–76 Teaching Session, Royal Victoria Hospital," *Ulster Medical Journal*, vol. 45, no. 1, 1976. www.ncbi.nlm.nih.gov /pmc/articles/PMC2385545/pdf/ulstermedj00112-0050.pdf.
50. Rossella Lorenzi, "Bad Teeth Tormented Ancient Egyptians," Discovery News, December 3, 2009. http://news.discovery.com.
51. Quoted in Mertz, *Red Land, Black Land*, p. 298.
52. Wilkinson, *The Rise and Fall of Ancient Egypt*, p. 39.
53. Quoted in *NOVA*, "Who Built the Pyramids?," PBS.org, February 4, 1997. www.pbs.org.
54. Mertz, *Red Land, Black Land*, p. 99.
55. Wilkinson, *The Rise and Fall of Ancient Egypt*, pp. 16–17.

CHAPTER FOUR: RELIGION AND THE AFTERLIFE

56. Herodotus, *Histories*, p. 134.
57. Mertz, *Red Land, Black Land*, p. 260.
58. Quoted in A.R. Williams, "Animal Mummies."
59. Wilkinson, *The Rise and Fall of Ancient Egypt*," p. 15.

60. Fletcher, *The Egyptian Book of Living and Dying*, p. 7.
61. Quoted in Fletcher, *The Egyptian Book of Living and Dying*, pp. 127–28.
62. Quoted in Ancient Egypt, "Personal Hygiene and Cosmetics."
63. Quoted in Thompson, *A History of Egypt*, p. 34.
64. Quoted in "The Afterlife in Ancient Egypt," *Nova*, January 3, 2006. www.pbs.org/wgbh/nova/ancient/afterlife-ancient-egypt.html
65. Quoted in *NOVA*, "The Afterlife in Ancient Egypt," PBS.org, January 3, 2006. www.pbs.org.
66. Hamilton, *The Greek Way*, p. 19.
67. Pierre Montet, *Everyday Life in Egypt in the Days of Ramesses the Great*, trans. A.R. Maxwell-Hyslop and Margaret S. Drower. Philadelphia: University of Pennsylvania Press, 1981, p. 330.
68. Thompson, *A History of Egypt*, p. 34.
69. Quoted in Humanistic Texts, "Ptahhotep."

FOR FURTHER RESEARCH

BOOKS

Margaret Bunson, *Encyclopedia of Ancient Egypt*. New York: Facts On File, 2012.

Joann Fletcher, *The Egyptian Book of Living and Dying*. London: Duncan Baird, 2009.

Herodotus, *The Landmark Herodotus: The Histories*. Edited by Robert B. Strassler. Translated by Andrea L. Purvis. (Reprint.) New York: Anchor, 2009.

Barbara Mertz, *Red Land, Black Land: Daily Life in Ancient Egypt*. New York: William Morrow, 2009.

Joyce Tyldesley, *The Pharaohs*. London: Quercus, 2009.

John Manchip White, *Everyday Life in Ancient Egypt*. Mineola, New York: Dover Publications, 2011.

Toby Wilkinson, *The Rise and Fall of Ancient Egypt*. New York: Random House, 2011.

WEBSITES

"A Day in the Life," *Egypt's Golden Empire* (www.pbs.org/empires /egypt/special/lifeas/index.html). Depicts daily lives of seven typical Egyptians, ranging from pharaoh to farmer.

Ancient Egypt (www.reshafim.org.il/ad/egypt/index.html). Very comprehensive website, with hundreds of topics and many contemporary citations.

Ancient Egypt (www.teacheroz.com/egypt.htm). Website prepared by an educator, with more than 100 links to sites covering virtually every aspect of Egyptian life.

Egyptian Life (www.ancientegypt.co.uk/life/home.html). British Museum website that includes information on daily life and playing senet, a popular ancient Egyptian board game.

Hydrology of the Nile (www.utdallas.edu/geosciences/remsens/Nile/Hydromap.html). University of Texas website that explains the variations in flow of the Nile River and shows month-by-month levels at five key locations.

Mysteries of Egypt (www.civilization.ca/cmc/exhibitions/civil/Egypt/egypte.shtml#menu). Website prepared by Canadian Museum of Civilization showing several aspects of daily life in ancient Egypt. Includes numerous illustrations.

Secrets of the Pharaohs, **PBS.org** (www.pbs.org/wnet/pharaohs). Website depicting the daily lives of five typical Egyptians: pharaoh, priestess, merchant, laborer, slave.

INDEX

Note: Boldface page numbers indicate illustrations.

afterlife
    animals in, 55, 59
    appearance in, 61, 64
    behavior in this life and, 60–61
    importance of, 60–61, 66–67
    medical care in, 56
    standard of living in, 66
    tomb robbers and, 63
    See also burials; mummification
agriculture. *See* farming
Akhenaten (pharaoh), 52, 67
Amenhotep III (pharaoh), 35, 50–52
Ammut, 60
amulets, 44, 60, 64
Amun (god), 56
Amun-Ra (god), 25, 56
animals
    burial of, 55, 59
    used by police, 42
Anubis (god), 60
Archimedes' screw, 53
army, 34
Assessors, 60

bathrooms, 17
beards, 24
beauty, **24**
    after death, 61, 64
    eyes, 23, 24
    facial hair, 16
    hair care, 21, 22, 23–24
    skin care, 16, 22–23, 45
beds, 18
beer, 20–21
Bes (god), 58
Black Land, 8
Blue Nile, 8–9
board games, 36
Book of the Dead, 61
brain and mummification, 62, **65**
bread, 19, **19**, 20, 47

bricks, 16, 20, 50
burials
    afterlife and, 43
    of animals, 55, 59
    locations, 60
    of poor, 66
    tomb robbers, 63
    See also mummification

calendar, 8, 45
Campbell, Jackie, 44, 45
canals, 17, 51, 52–53
capital punishment, 42–43, 63
carpenters, 29
celebrations, 28, 37–38
chariot corps, 34
childbirth, 15, 16, 58
children
    age at marriage, 13, 14
    care of, 16
    clothing for, 22
    education of, 48
    on farms, 13, 27
    gods to protect, 58
    hairstyles of boys, 22
    love of, 13
    mortality rate, 15–16
    preference for boys, 13–14
    toys and games of, 36–37
cleanliness
    home, 16, 17
    personal, 17, 18, 22, 24, 47–48, 62
clothing, 21–22, 28
crime, 42
crocodiles, 36, 55, 60

dancing, 15, 31, 38, 48
Deir-el-Medina, 20
deities. *See* religion
dentistry, 46–48, 56
deret (Red Land), 8, 11
diet, 19–21, **19**, 47
Dog Star, 6
Dornbusch, Horst, 20–21

PICTURE CREDITS

Cover: The Subsiding of the Nile, 1873 (oil on canvas) - © Russell-Cotes Art Gallery and Museum, Bournemouth, UK

© Nathan Benn/Corbis: 12

© Gianni Dagli Orti/Corbis: 57

© Blue Lantern Studio/Corbis: 43

Borromeo / Art Resource, NY: 51

Werner Forman / Art Resource, NY: 19

Erich Lessing / Art Resource, NY: 24, 27

© National Geographic Society/Corbis: 33

SSPL/Science Museum/Art Resource, NY: 65

Thinkstock/iStockphotos.com: 5 (bottom left), 7

ABOUT THE AUTHOR

Jim Whiting has published more than 130 nonfiction books for young readers. He has also edited nearly 200 titles among many genres. His diverse career includes 17 years publishing *Northwest Runner* magazine, advising a national award–winning high school newspaper, hundreds of venue and event descriptions and photography for America Online, serving as sports editor for the *Bainbridge Island Review*, and writing hundreds of articles for newspapers and magazines throughout the country.